Y0-BEO-132

Lover's Knot Placemats

Cynthia Martin

a Quilt in a Day Publication

To my Husband, Jon,
the love of my life with whom I "tied the knot"
and to my family who have always supported me.

Published by Quilt in a Day, Inc.

1955 Diamond Street, San Marcos, CA 92069

Copyright © 1993 by Cynthia Martin

First Printing November 1993

ISBN -0-922705-45-3

Editor Eleanor Burns

Art Direction Merritt Voigtlander

Printed in the United States of America on recycled paper. All rights reserved. No part of this material may be reproduced in any form or by any electronic or mechanical means, including information storage and retrieval systems, without permission in writing from the author.

Contents

Getting acquainted

Choosing Fabrics

Select four different fabric values for your Lover's Knot Placemats:

- Dark medium
- Light
- Light Medium
- Dark

When choosing fabrics, the Dark and Dark Medium create two different blocks so they should be dominant. Choose fabrics that have different sizes of print or add solids.

- The triangles are made from the same Light fabric that is in the blocks
- Border #1 is made from any fabric color except the Dark
- Border #2 is made from the Dark fabric

Backing

- Match the backing to the Dark border fabric
- Use 100% cotton, 45" wide fabrics

Batting

Use 3 oz. bonded batting or fleece. Fleece is slightly more dense than bonded batting and is often used in quilted clothing and pot holders.

Fabric Preparation

Prewash all fabrics prior to cutting to prevent shrinkage. You may want to spray your finished placemats with Scotchguard™.

¼" Accurate Seams

An accurate and consistent ¼" seam is very important. The smaller a project is the more important the accuracy becomes. Pay close attention to your seam allowance as you sew. Use a magnetic seam guide or a guide made from foot and shoe padding. The foot and shoe padding is an extra-thick latex foam with a self-stick adhesive. It comes in 7" x 3⅜" packages which can be cut to approximately ¼" x 1". Place it ¼" from the needle position.

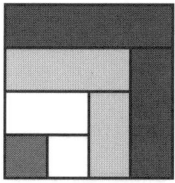 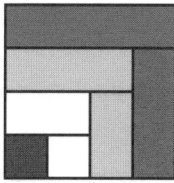

A Block   *B Block*

Paste-up Page

Cut and paste fabric pieces on the Paste-up blocks and in the boxes. You will see how your fabrics work together.

Dark Medium

Light

Light Medium

Dark

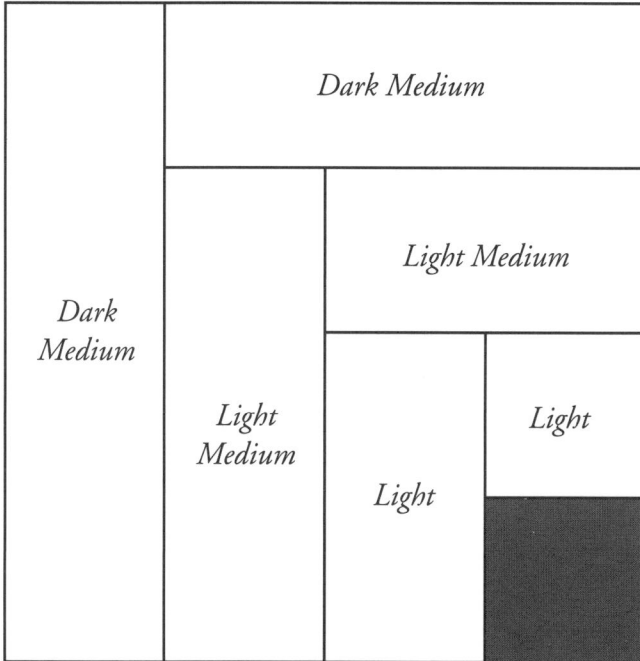

B Block

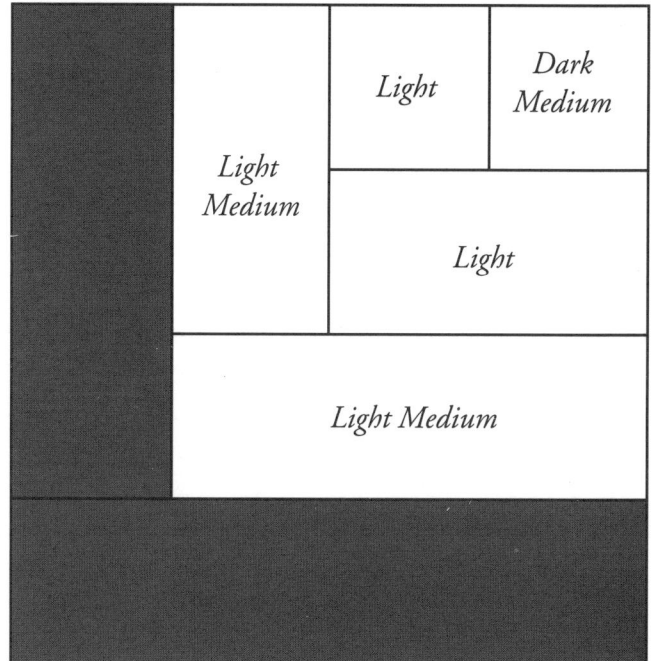

A Block

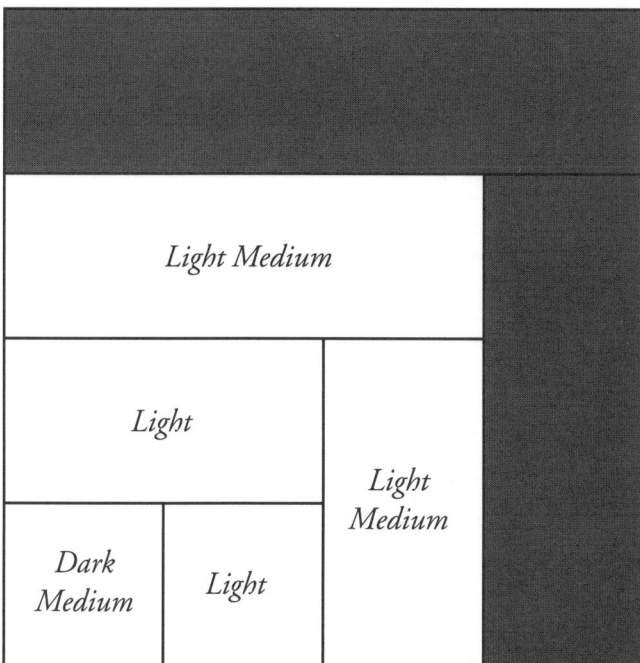

A Block

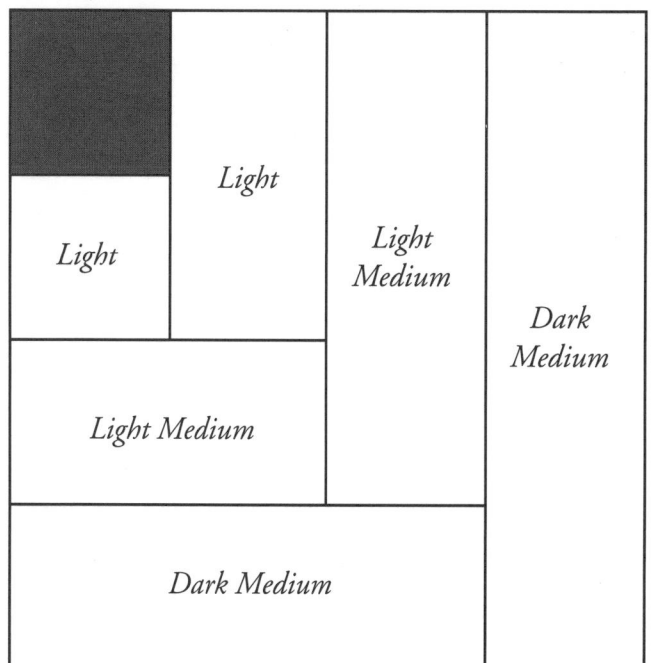

B Block

Yardage for six placemats

Fabric	Yardage	Cut strips selvage to selvage
Dark Medium	¼ yd	*four* 1½" *wide strips*
Light	¾ yd	*six* 1½" *wide strips*
Light Triangles		*two* 7½" *wide strips*
Light Medium	⅜ yd	*eight* 1½" *wide strips*
Dark	½ yd	*nine* 1½" *wide strips*
1st Border *any fabric except dark*	½ yd	*ten* 1½" *wide strips*
2nd Border *dark*	½ yd	*eleven* 1½" *wide strips*
Batting *fleece or 3oz.*	1½ yds	*six* 17" x 22" *pieces*
Backing *same as 2nd border*	1½ yds	*six* 17" x 22" *pieces*

Supplies

Rotary cutter

Magnetic seam guide

Invisible thread   Thread

Point turner

Walking foot

Extra long quilting pins

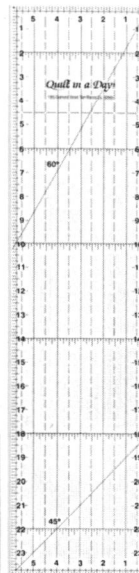
6" x 24"

6" x 6"

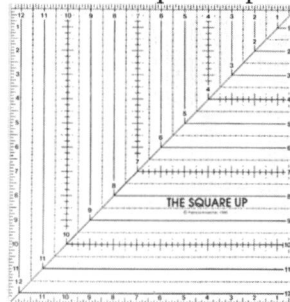
12 ½" Square Up

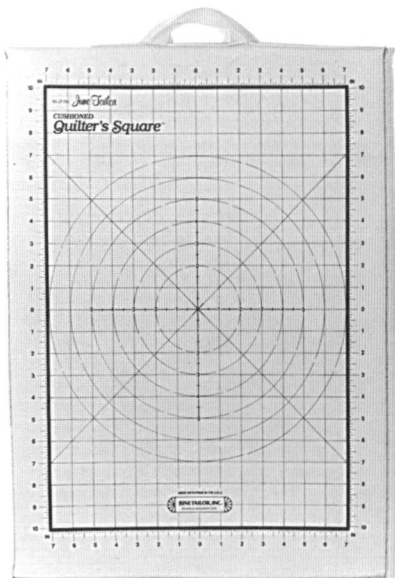
Pressing Mat

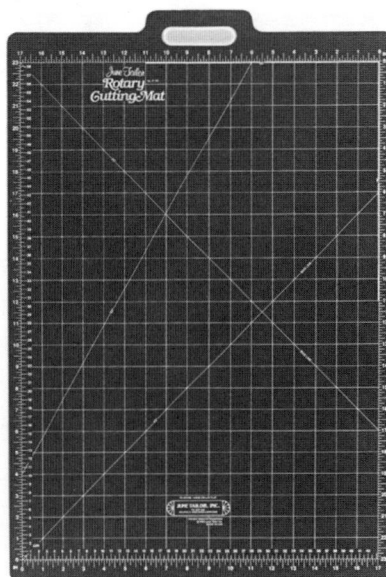
Cutting mat

General Cutting Directions

Use a rotary cutter and 6" x 24" plexiglass ruler for cutting strips. Use a 12½" Square Up ruler for cuttings strips into squares. Use a 6" x 6" plexiglass ruler for cutting blocks apart.

Reverse the following procedure if you are left handed.

Cutting Strips

1. Make a nick on the edge of your fabric and tear from selvage to selvage. This will put the fabric on the straight-of-grain.

2. Fold the fabric in half, matching the torn edge.

3. With the fold of the fabric at the bottom, lay fabric on the mat with most of it lying to the right.

4. Spread the fingers of your left hand to hold the ruler firmly. With the rotary cutter in your right hand, begin cutting with the blade off the fabric on the mat. Cut away from you and trim off the torn edge.

5. Lift and move the ruler over until the ruler lines are at the freshly cut edge. Carefully and accurately line up and cut the strips at 1½"or 7½".

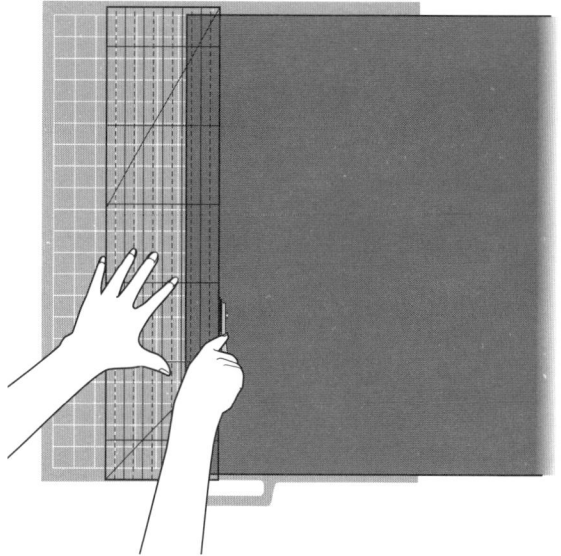

Cutting 7½" Light Strips into 7½" Squares

1. With the strip still folded, place the strip on the cutting mat grid line and square off the selvage ends.

2. Cut (9) 7½"squares from the strips.

Cutting the Triangles

Cut the squares into fourths diagonally. Stack right side up.

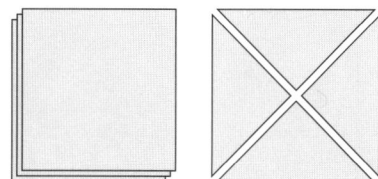

It takes two

Sewing 36 "A" Blocks

1. Cut one Light strip and one Dark Medium strip in half. Set a half strip of each aside for "B" block.

2. Count out an additional Light and Dark Medium strip.

3. Flip Dark Medium half strip right sides together onto Light half strip. Sew with an accurate ¼" seam allowance. Repeat with the pair of whole strips.

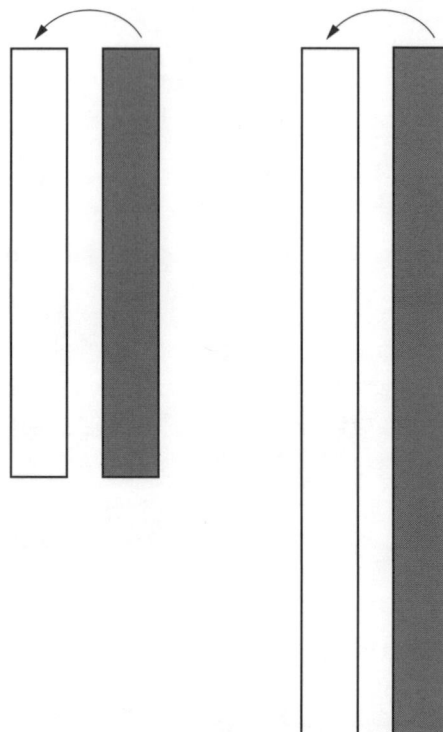

4. Lay sewn strip on cutting mat. Lay ruler line on stitching line, and square off end using 6" x 6" ruler and rotary cutter.

5. Cut (36) 1½" squares.

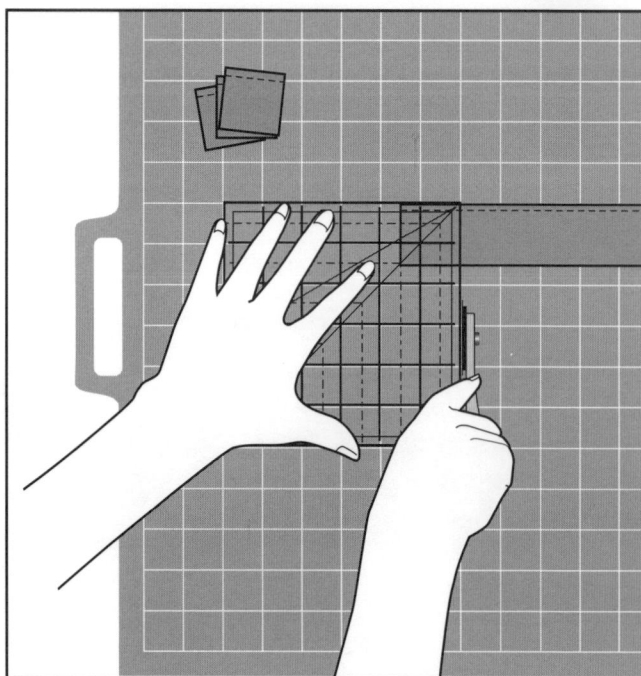

6. Open and stack blocks right side down next to your machine with the Light strip along the top.

7. Place a Light strip under sewing machine needle, right side up. Put the presser foot down to hold the fabric in place.

8. Place block right sides together on strip with Light end away from you. Sew about an inch to anchor block. Push the seam allowance toward the Light fabric. Pull the end of the block and continue to sew to within 1" of end. Make sure that there are no puckers or folds at the seam as you sew over it.

9. Add next block, butting the two together.

10. Continue in this manner until all blocks are used.

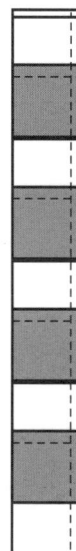

11. Lay strips on cutting mat along a grid line. Place a 6" x 6" ruler on top of strip and cut between blocks, trimming where necessary.

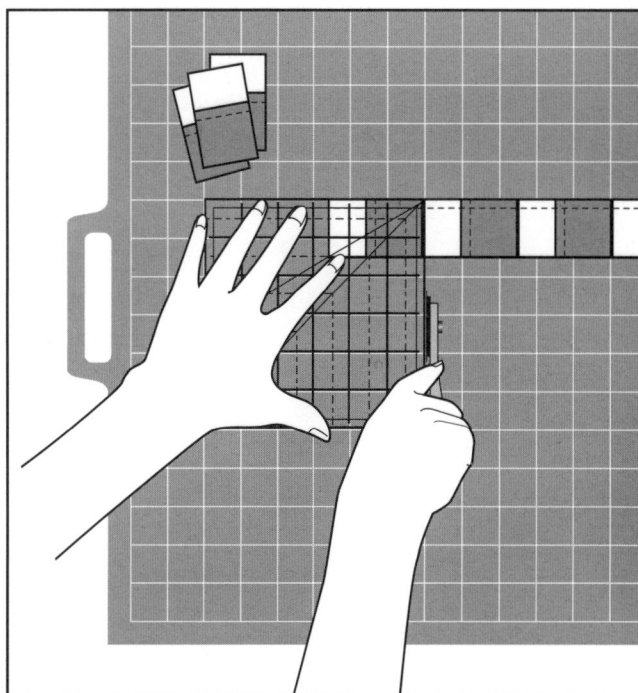

Adding Light Medium Strips to the "A" Blocks

1. Open and stack blocks right side down next to machine with the Light strip along the bottom.

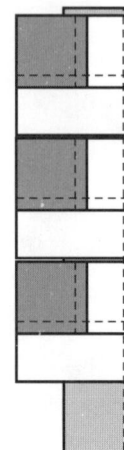

2. Place a Light Medium strip under needle, right side up.

3. Place block right sides together on strip with Light strip of block near you. Anchor and pull block as before watching out for puckers and folds. Push the seam allowance toward the Light fabric.

4. Sew, butting blocks together. Continue until all blocks are used.

5. Cut apart, trimming where necessary.

6. Open and stack the blocks right side down next to machine with the Light Medium strip toward the top.

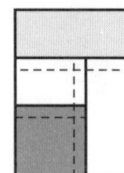

7. Place a Light Medium strip under needle, right side up.

8. Place a block right sides together on strip with Light Medium strip of block away from you. Anchor and pull block, pushing the seam allowance toward the Light Medium fabric.

9. Sew, butting blocks together. Continue until all blocks are used.

10. Cut apart, trimming where necessary.

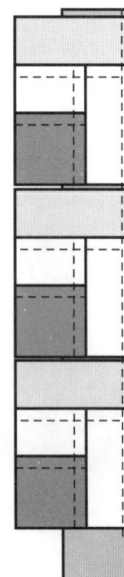

Adding Dark Strips to the "A" Blocks

1. Open and stack blocks right side down next to machine with Light Medium strip along the bottom.

2. Place a Dark strip under needle, right side up.

3. Place block right sides together on strip with Light Medium strip of block near you. Anchor and pull block, pushing the seam allowance toward the Light Medium fabric.

4. Sew, butting blocks together. Continue until all blocks are used.

5. Cut apart, trimming where necessary.

6. Open and stack the blocks right side down next to machine with the Dark strip toward the top.

7. Place a Dark strip under needle, right side up.

8. Place a block right sides together on strip with Dark strip of block away from you. Anchor and pull block, pushing the seam allowance toward the Dark fabric.

9. Sew, butting blocks together. Continue until all blocks are used.

10. Cut apart, trimming where necessary.

11. Press the "A" Blocks. All seams should be pressed toward the Dark strips. Use a gridded pressing mat to keep the blocks square.

12. Stack right side up, and set the "A" Blocks aside for later use.

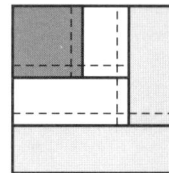

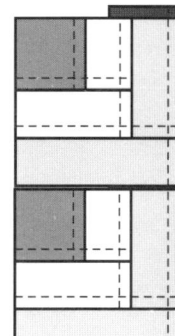

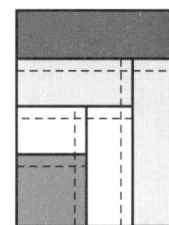

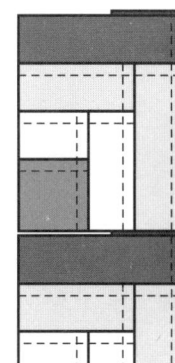

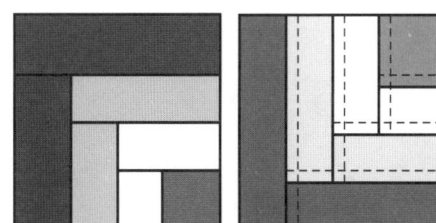

Sewing 12 "B" Blocks

Cut one Dark strip in half and use reserved Light half strip.

1. Flip Dark strip onto Light strip. Sew.

2. Lay sewn strip on cutting mat. Square off end using 6" x 6" ruler and rotary cutter.

3. Cut (12) 1½" squares.

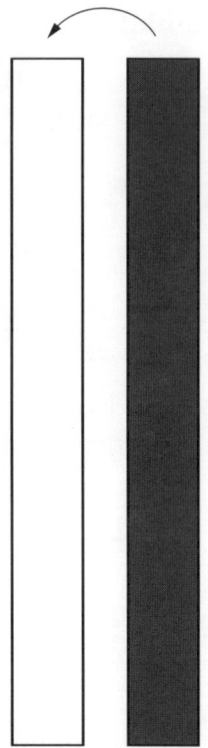

4. Open and stack blocks right side down next to your machine with the Light strip along the top.

5. Place a Light strip under needle, right side up.

6. Place block right sides together on strip with Light strip of block away from you. Anchor and pull block, pushing the seam allowance toward the Light fabric.

7. Sew, butting blocks together. Continue until all blocks are used.

8. Lay strips on cutting mat, and cut between blocks, trimming where necessary.

Adding Light Medium Strips to the "B" Blocks

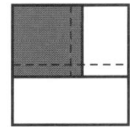

1. Open and stack blocks right side down next to machine with the Light strip along the bottom.

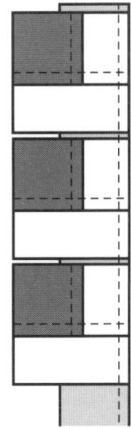

2. Place a Light Medium strip under needle, right side up.

3. Place block right sides together on strip with Light strip near you. Anchor and pull block, pushing the seam allowance toward the Light fabric.

4. Sew, butting blocks together. Continue until all blocks are used.

5. Cut apart, trimming where necessary.

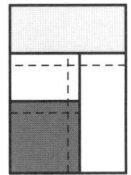

6. Open and stack the blocks right side down next to machine with the Light Medium strip toward the top.

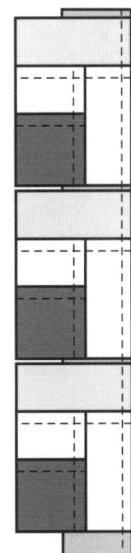

7. Place a Light Medium strip under needle, right side up.

8. Place a block right sides together on strip with Light Medium strip of block away from you. Anchor and pull block, pushing the seam allowance toward the Light Medium fabric.

9. Sew, butting blocks together. Continue until all blocks are used.

10. Cut apart, trimming where necessary.

Adding Dark Medium Strips to the "B" Blocks

1. Open and stack the blocks right side down next to machine with Light Medium fabric toward the bottom.

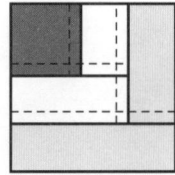

2. Place a Dark Medium strip under needle, right side up.

3. Place block right sides together on strip with Light Medium strip of block near you. Push seam allowance toward the Light Medium fabric.

4. Sew, butting blocks together. Continue until all blocks are used.

5. Cut apart, trimming where necessary.

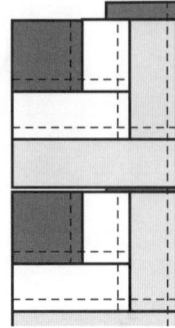

6. Open and stack the blocks right side down next to machine with the Dark Medium strip toward the top.

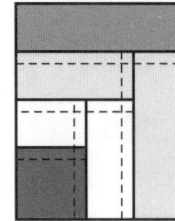

7. Place a Dark Medium strip under needle, right side up.

8. Place a block right sides together on strip with Dark Medium strip of block away from you.

9. Sew, butting blocks together. Continue until all blocks are used.

10. Cut apart, trimming where necessary.

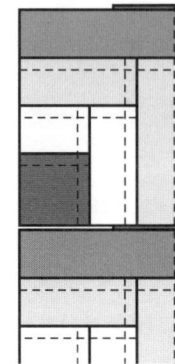

11. Press the "B" blocks. All the seams should be pressed toward the Dark Medium strips. Use a gridded pressing mat to keep the blocks square.

12. Stack "B" Blocks right side up.

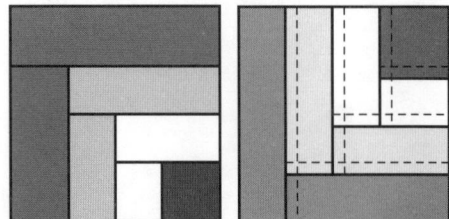

Sewing Six "Center Knot" Blocks

The Center Knot is made from "A" and "B" blocks.

Stack up two piles of six each of the "A" and "B" blocks. Arrange them so that all the darks come together and the "A" blocks are opposite each other. Place the stacks next to your sewing machine.

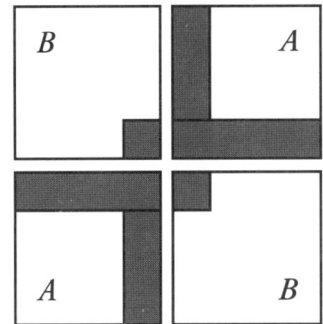

1. Flip the right block onto the left block. Match the pressed seams as you sew across them.

2. Assembly-line sew, butting the pairs together.

3. Pull the connecting threads for some length. Flip and sew the remaining pairs.

4. Clip the threads between sets of Center Knots. Open and stack.

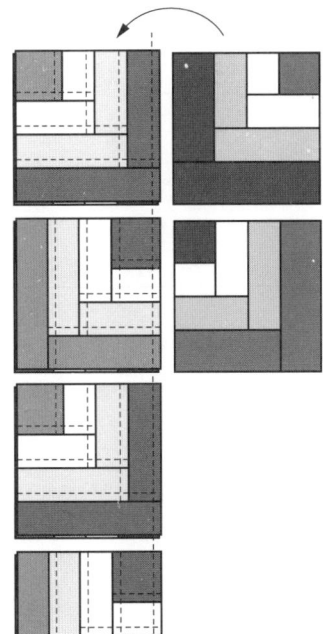

5. Rotate stack 90 degrees.

6. Flip the right set onto the left set.

7. Match seams as you sew across them, pushing center seams in opposite directions.

8. Clip the threads between sets of Center Knots.

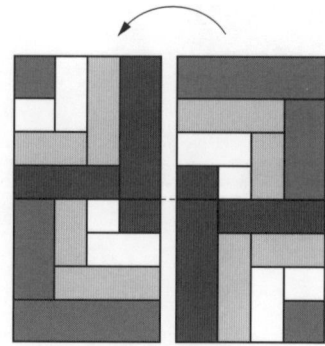

9. Press the "Center Knot" blocks.

10. Stack the "Center Knots" and set aside for later use.

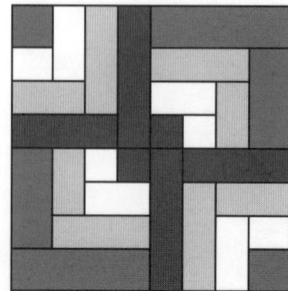

Sewing "A" Block and Single Triangle

Triangles are oversized. Triangle tips will hang over the edges of the blocks.

1. Stack 12 "A" blocks with the Medium Dark corner of the "A" block in the upper left corner. Place a stack of 12 triangles to the right of the "A" blocks.

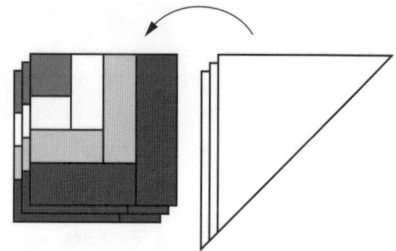

2. Flip one Triangle onto one "A" block right sides together. Match up straight tops and right edges. Do not stretch the triangles. Sew. Do not clip connecting threads. Triangle tips hang over.

3. Continue in this manner until all blocks are used.

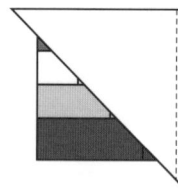

4. Clip connecting threads.

5. Press seams toward the triangle.

6. Put the "A" and Single Triangle blocks aside for later use.

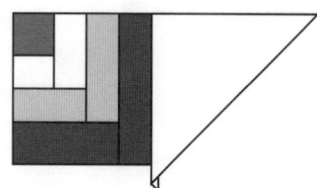

Sewing "A" Block and Double Triangle

1. Make a stack of 12 "A" blocks with the Dark Medium square in the upper right corner. Place stacks of 12 triangles to the right and left.

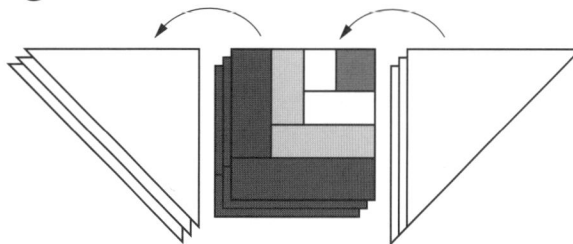

2. Flip one "A" block onto one of the left hand stacks of triangles, right sides together. Sew. Do not stretch the triangles. Do not cut connecting threads.

3. Continue in this manner until all blocks are used.

4. Clip the connecting threads.

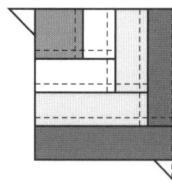

5. Flip a triangle right sides together onto an "A" block. Sew. Do not stretch the triangles. Do not cut connecting threads. Continue in this manner until all blocks are used.

6. Clip the connecting threads.

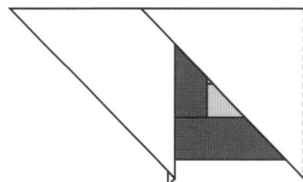

7. Press seams toward triangles.

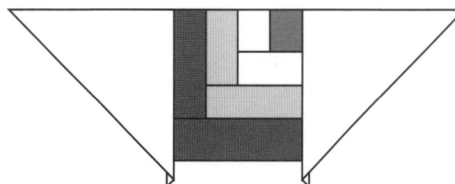

Setting the Blocks Together

1. Lay out the pieces. Stack piles of 6 each. Double check the position of the Dark fabric.

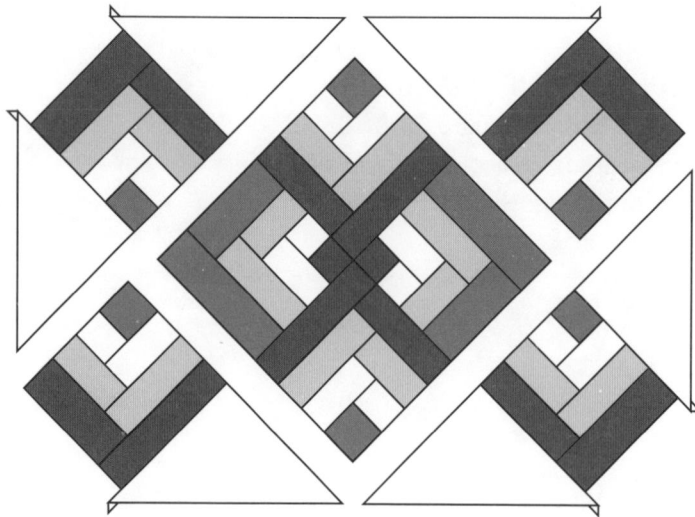

2. Sew an "A" block and Single Triangle to both sides of a Center Knot. Match square edges and seams. Fingerpress seams in opposite directions.

3. Press towards the Center Knot.

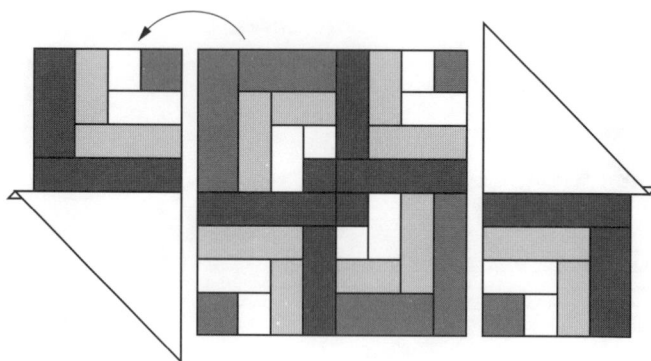

4. Sew an "A" block and Double Triangle to both sides of the Center Knot.

5. Press seams toward the outside edge.

6. Repeat for all placemats.

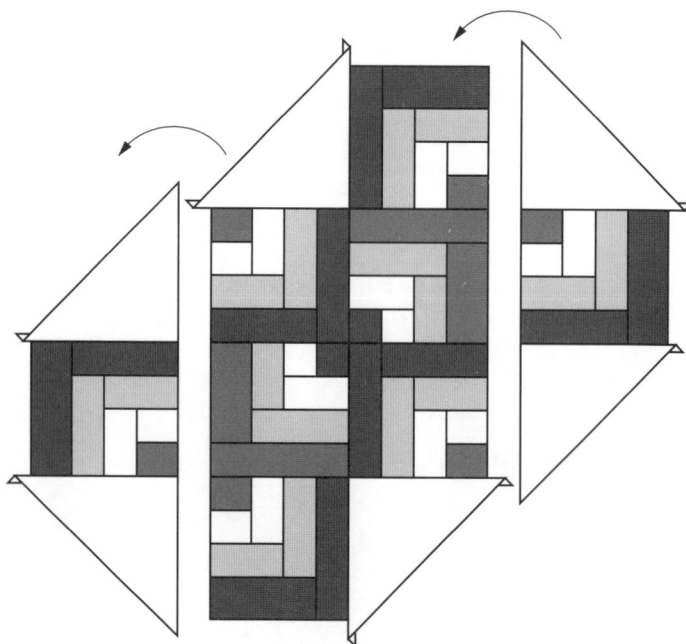

Trimming excess triangle fabric

1. There will be some excess triangle fabric that needs to be trimmed away. Place a 6" x 24" ruler along the long edge of your placemat so that the edges of the ruler touch the corners.

2. Place the ruler's ¼" line on the Center Knot point.

3. Trim the excess triangle fabric away. Be careful not to trim away the ¼" seam allowance.

4. Trim the other long edge.

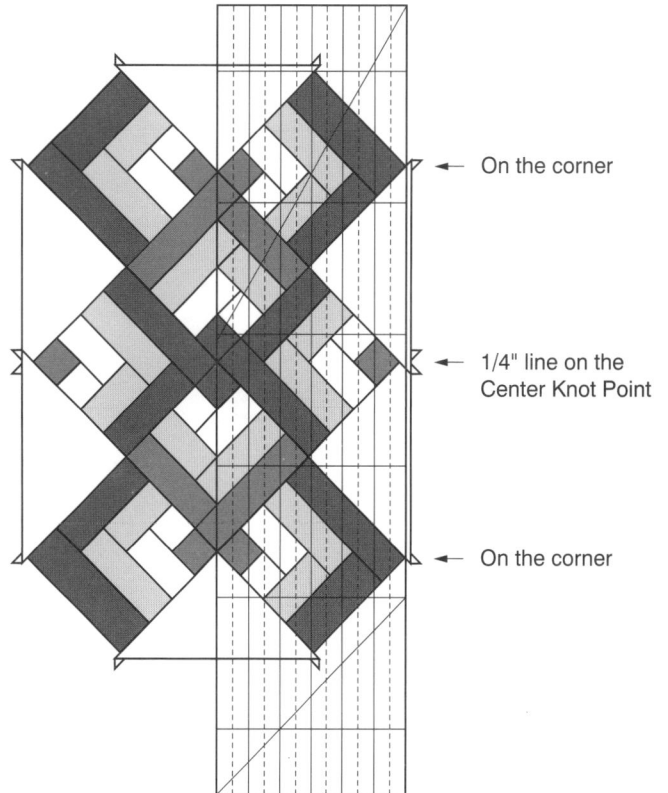

← On the corner

← 1/4" line on the Center Knot Point

← On the corner

5. Place a 6" x 24" ruler along the short edge of your placemat so that the edges touch the corners.

6. Trim the excess triangle fabric. Trim the other short edge.

7. Place a 6" x 24" ruler along the corner of your placemat so that the edges touch the corners.

8. Trim the excess triangle fabric. Trim the other corners.

9. Repeat for all placemats.

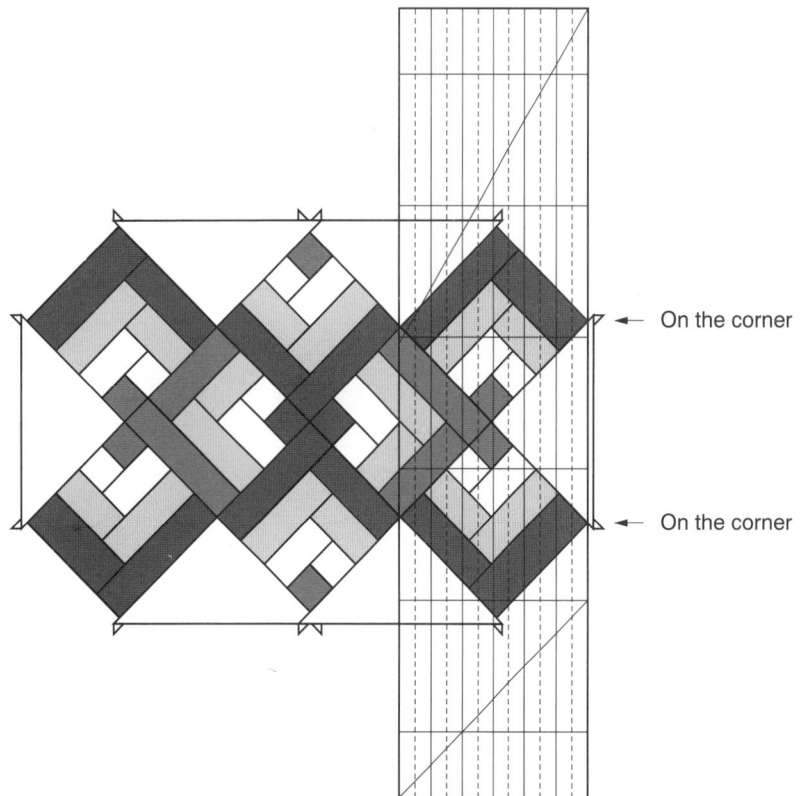

← On the corner

← On the corner

A dream comes true

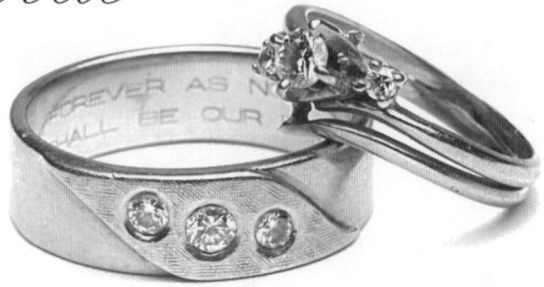

Borders

First Border

1. Place a First Border strip under sewing machine needle.

2. Place long side of placemat right side down on strip, about ½" from end of strip.

3. Sew border to both long sides of all placemats.

4. Sew border to both ends of all placemats.

5. Open and press seams toward border strips.

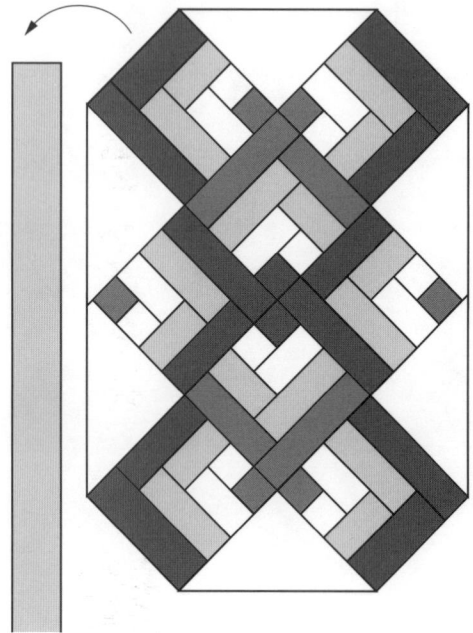

6. Place the 6" x 24" ruler across the corner. Trim excess with rotary cutter.

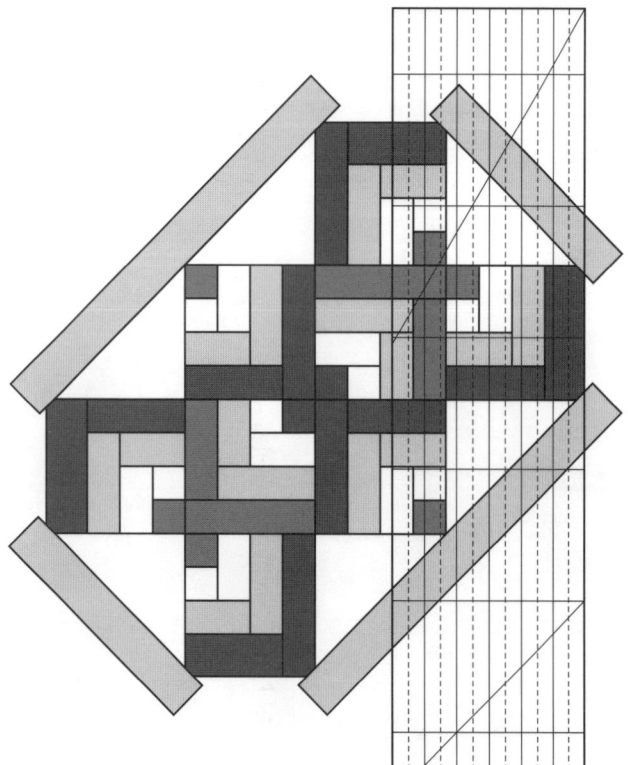

7. Sew border strips to remaining diagonal corners.

8. Open and press seams toward border strips.

9. Trim excess with rotary cutter.

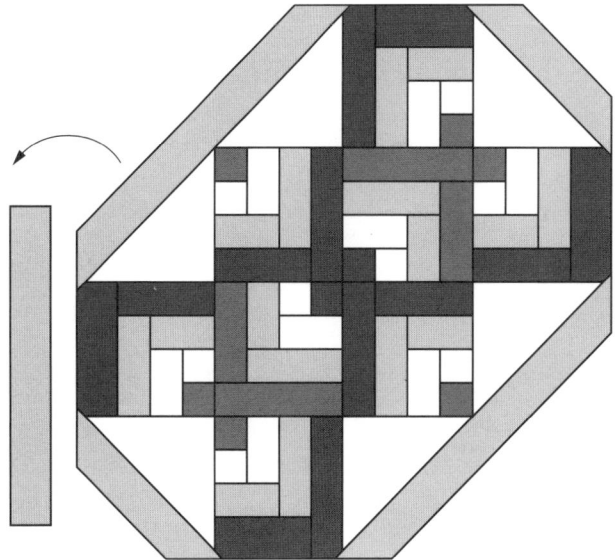

Second Border

1. Place Second Border strip under sewing machine needle.

2. Place a long side of placemat right side down on strip.

3. Sew border to both long sides of all placemats.

4. Sew border to both ends of all placemats.

5. Open and press seams toward border strips.

6. Trim away excess with rotary cutter.

7. Sew border strips to remaining diagonal corners.

8. Open and press seams toward border strips.

9. Trim away excess border strip.

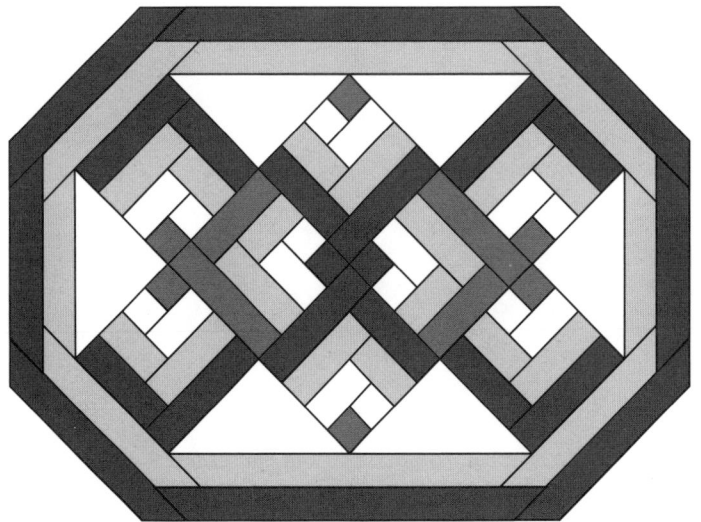

Finishing

Cutting the Backing and Batting

1. Cut six 17" x 22" pieces of backing.

2. Cut six 17" x 22" pieces of batting or fleece.

Quick Turn

1. Lay batting down flat.

2. Lay backing fabric on top of batting right side up.

3. Lay placemat right sides together on top of backing.

4. Make sure that the backing and placemat are lying flat.

5. Pin around the outside edge of the placemat through all layers.

6. Sew ¼" around the outside edge leaving a 5" opening along the middle of one long side for turning.

7. Trim away excess batting and backing along the ¼" seam allowance. Do not trim near the opening.

8. Turn right side out through the opening. Use a point turner to poke out corners.

9. Slip stitch the opening closed.

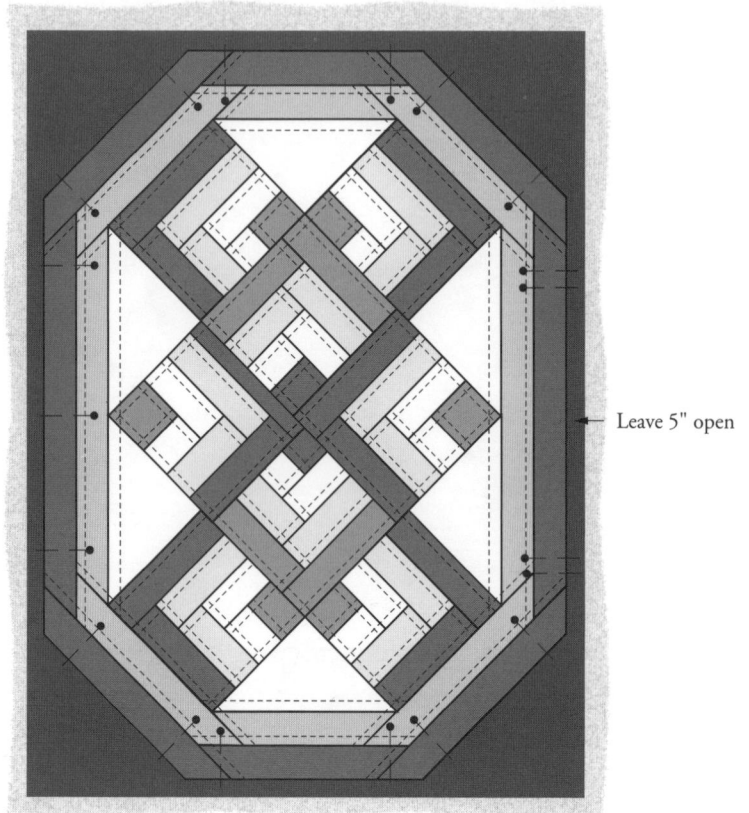

← Leave 5" open

Machine Quilting

1. Place quilting pins along the lines of the individual blocks and along each border.

2. Use 10 stitches per inch or a #3 setting.

3. Use a walking foot.

4. Use regular thread to match your backing in the bobbin and invisible thread and a fine needle for the upper stitches.

5. "Stitch in the ditch" where each of the blocks meet and around each border.

Acknowledgements

My thanks to Eleanor Burns for her help in writing this publication, and for the original idea which came from her book, *Lover's Knot Quilt.*

I am grateful to all of my students who had a hand in helping to develop this publication.

My sincere thanks to students and friends who loaned china, placemats, and silverware for the cover photos.

Order Information

Quilt in a Day books offer a wide range of techniques and are directed toward a variety of skill levels. If you do not have a quilt shop in your area, you may write for a complete catalog and current price list of all books and patterns published by Quilt in a Day®, Inc., 1955 Diamond Street, San Marcos, CA 92069 or call 1(760)591-0081 or order toll free 1(800)777-4852

Easy

These books are easy enough for beginners of any age.
Log Cabin Quilt in a Day
Irish Chain
Trip Around the World
Heart's Delight
Scrap Quilt
Rail Fence
Dresden Placemats
Flying Geese
Star for all Seasons

Applique

While these books offer a variety of techniques, easy applique is featured in each.
Dresden Plate
Sunbonnet Sue Visits Quilt in a Day
Recycled Treasures
Creating with Color
Spools & Tools

Intermediate to Advanced

With a little Quilt in a Day experience, these books offer a rewarding project.
Trio
Lover's Knot
Amish Quilt
May Basket
Morning Star
Friendship Quilt
Tulip Quilt
Burgoyne Surrounded
Snowball
Tulip Table Runner

Holiday

When a favorite holiday is approaching, Quilt in a Day is there to help you plan.
Country Christmas
Bunnies & Blossoms
Patchwork Santa
Last Minute Gifts
Angel of Antiquity
Log Cabin Wreath
Log Cabin Tree
Country Flag

Sampler

Always and forever popular are books with a variety of patterns.
The Sampler
Block Party Series 1, Quilter's Year
Block Party Series 2, Baskets and Flowers
Block Party Series 3, Quilters' Almanac
Block Party Series 4, Christmas Traditions
Block Party Series 5, Pioneer Sampler

Angle Piecing

Quilt in a Day "template free" methods make angle cutting less of a challenge.
Schoolhouse
Diamond Log Cabin
Pineapple Quilt
Radiant Star
Blazing Star Tablecloth